The

Dream Job

Secret

by Vincent Dolliole Jr.

Cover art designed by Amber Feldkamp

To Lillie Simmons, with love.

Contents

Disclaimer

The views expressed in this book are the author's own and do not reflect those of Victoria's Secret, L Brands, or any of it's affiliates.

Chapter 1

Why Listen To Me?

"The impossible becomes possible if only your mind believes it."

- Chris Bradford

*I'*m a straight male Victoria's Secret

employee. My job is to help women of all ages find the panties and bras they want, while at the same time creating for them a memorable experience with the customer service, which inspires them to return to our store.

Now, unlike most places, where I work provides more chances for things to get weird. Such as this one time towards the beginning of working there. I was on the register, and I was just about done with a transaction. I was checking out a woman, and had put all of her items in the bag. Everything about the checkout was smooth, until I placed the receipt in the bag and handed it to her.

As I gave her a "thanks for coming in, have a nice day" she had the most puzzled look on her face. Before I could ask her what was up, she said it.

"Can I touch your face?"

My eyes went big. I tried my best to come up with something, but I'm pretty sure it just resulted in a few seconds of awkward eye contact between us. I was really caught off guard by her question. What do you say to something like that?

I think I managed to get out a confused "Ummmm....."

As I was still in shock from what she just asked me, she didn't bother waiting for my response.

The woman literally reached over the counter, grabbed my face, said "thank you," and left.

My manager thought it was pretty funny and teased me by grabbing her face for the rest of that day. That's just a taste of the things I deal with on a daily. Throughout this book you will have the chance to read about even more of my crazy experiences I've had at work.

I have had such a significant amount of people ask me to explain how I got my job, that I've decided to answer that frequently asked question in this book.

How cool would that be for someone to ask me "You work at Victoria's Secret? Dude...how did you manage that?" and I would be able to reply with "Oh you can read all about it in my book." "You have a book too?? How old are you?" It's a conversation starter in itself.

Chapter 2

Becoming An Angel

"Starting right now, attempt to live as if you have no regrets."
-John O'Callaghan

*A*s shocking as it may sound, I wasn't just born a world class panty folder.

This will probably be the last time I ever explain this before I just start telling people, "You can read all about it in my book."

My whole life I've loved technology, and always knew I would probably end up with a career in engineering or science. If a year ago you had told me I would end up selling bras at Victoria's Secret, I would have most likely laughed in your face. I had just recently graduated high school just months earlier, and the thought of more ~~prison~~ school was definitely unappealing.

So I took a year break off from signing up for college classes to work, travel a bit, and do whatever else I desired. I wasn't quite sure what I wanted to do with my life just yet, but for the moment, college wasn't one of them.

Now, on to how I came to be....not birth, my employment.

One day in October, I decided I wanted to go to Texas. So, I did what any action taking person would do and bought myself a plane ticket at five in the morning, & got a friend who lived about 10 miles away to wake up her mom to drive me to the airport. While I waited for them to arrive at my house, I packed anything I might need, snuck out of the house through the garage while everyone was sleeping, and we left for the airport.

I almost missed my flight, not because of any time shortage, but simply due to my own confusion. People were upset after they woke up and I was in Houston, but things quickly began to calm down and I made the last flight to Corpus Christi, Texas. I always enjoyed flying there, because I would always end up on a jet.

A week after I got there, I applied for a job at a few places. One of them, being the Coach store. I walked in asking for an interview, and they really liked me and said to come back the next day.

So I did, but I was two minutes late, so I just didn't show up. I figured, if I can't be on time, why even bother to show up? Plus, I was honestly just hungry and wanted to get home.

The next day I walked into Victoria's Secret and filled out an application. I got hired.

I still remember the moment. I was inside, using my laptop on my bed when I got the call. I knew who it was because from the interviewing I had saved the store's number in my phone. I picked up my phone to see who was calling me and when I looked at it, it read "La Palmera Victoria's Secret." My eyes went big.

I answered the phone "Hello?"

A woman said "Hi, this is Lupe from Victoria's Secret. Is this Vincent?"

I confirmed.

"I'm calling to offer you a cashier position, do you accept the offer?"

I accepted.

"Great, welcome to Victoria's Secret. You handsome, charming, well dressed...."

Okay, so maybe that last part's not exactly how she said it, but I like to think that's how it happened.

Naturally, all the women in my family got excited when they heard the news. Most of them have pretty big mouths, so it didn't take long for word to spread. I also had to explain to my grandpa why he couldn't just come into the store to take pictures of me at my new job. I still don't think he realizes how bad that sounded.

Chapter 3

The Application Process

"To get a step up in the world, you could use a ladder, or you could use your connections. I prefer the latter."
-Jarod Kintz

*Y*our best chance at getting the job is to be able to talk to someone face to face, and share your amazing personality with to make yourself memorable. Unfortunately, most places nowadays do their applications online. So you can thank the technological advancements of society for making your efforts harder than what they already are.

When I applied, I walked right in and asked the girl at the counter for an application. I honestly wasn't afraid like most guys, and didn't even think much of it. She was more than happy to give me one, and told me I could fill it out and then come to an interview that was being held about a couple hours later.

I went to the food court to fill out the application, before returning to the store to get a new one after messing up in pen. I then turned it in and took off to roam the mall, window shopping as I waited for the interview to start.

Although paper applications have just about suffered the same fate as Blockbuster, it's best to ask if the place you are applying to has paper applications available. If so, you should also ask when you might be able to come back in for an interview. Filling out and turning in a paper application helps you to stand out a little more than submitting your application and resume to the online "black hole" of applicants.

The girl who gave me my application told me before I could even ask, but it never hurts to ask when a possible interview could happen. It also lets them know how serious you are.

I also did this when I almost applied at the Coach store in the mall, and they loved me, so they asked me to come in the following day.

Like most people say, it's not what you know, but who you know. This is absolutely true. So if you know someone in a position to help you out, you have a much higher chance of getting hired. Especially if you're applying online.

Since I was new to the city, I knew almost no one, but I'm like awesome so of course I still got it. Definitely no sarcasm here.

Chapter 4

Pre-Interview

"By failing to prepare, you are preparing to fail."
- Benjamin Franklin

I didn't have time to prepare for the first interview since mine was only a few hours after applying, but yours is not likely to be as soon.

No matter what skills you have, or how colorful your resume is, it doesn't matter how good you look on paper if you aren't able to present yourself professionally in an interview.

To prepare, it's good to do mock interviews. Have someone you know act as the interviewer and go over questions most likely to be asked. They will be able to help you really get your answers down and with any problems you may have interviewing.

Chapter 5

Dress Attire

"Dress for the job you want,
not the one you have."

For the interview, you should dress as if you already have the job and are coming in not for an interview, but a shift.

Take notice of what the employees are wearing and follow suit. Even if the interview is casual, I still advise you dress up. Aim to be the best looking person in that room.

For my first interview, I didn't have any time to head home and change what I was wearing. For the second interview I had time, but I didn't have any examples of what a male employee might wear, due to not seeing any at the time and there being no such results in a Google search.

I took the dress code colors I saw the employees wearing, and figured out an outfit to throw together.

When I walked into the store for my second interview, I was immediately by a women shopper who thought I worked there.

Lacking the training I was there to receive, I had no choice but to turn her over to someone else. That interaction with her confirmed I had nailed the "look," and I made sure to mention to the hiring manager how I had just been mistaken for an employee walking in.

She seemed to like that.

<u>Guys</u>
- Be well groomed
  (Haircut, shower, deodorant, etc.)
- Smell good
  (You want them to invite you back)
- Make sure everything fits
  (No matter how much a suit costs, you're not going to look good if it looks like you're wearing an over-sized hand me down.)
- Please don't wear pants with pleats in them, especially khaki's.
  (Can't stress this enough.)

<u>Girls</u>
- Be well groomed
- Make sure everything fits
- Don't show up wearing leggings or yoga pants (A.K.A. lazy wear)
- Don't over do it. You don't want to show up looking like you're on the way to your senior prom.

Chapter 6

Dominating The Interview

"The need for anything gets in the way of everything."

I hate interviews. That being said, I've been through a ton. On the day of the interview it's good to get there about 15 minutes early.

This way you have plenty of time to get lost and find your way.

Skills

Not only have the necessary skills for the job, but also a variety of additional skills that may be useful. There are a number of online courses you can take to learn just about anything in your spare time, whether you're on the go or at home.

A lot of them take very little time to gain, and you can add them to your resume. One extremely useful website for this would be Udemy.

Group Interviews

It has become increasingly popular, and efficient for employers to hold what are known as group interviews. Instead of just a 1 on 1 interview with the employer, you will be interviewing alongside about 7 other applicants all at the same time.

When waiting, it's good to get to know and talk to the other applicants a little to get more comfortable with each other. You are going to be working with some of these people, so it looks good to your employer to see you've already met the others and are making friends with them.

<u>Body Language</u>

Look the interviewer in the eyes.

So many people shoot themselves in the foot by not doing this, as if eye contact is too much for them to handle.

Keep eye contact with who you're talking to. You stare them right into the deepest part of their soul. Which reminds me of one time I was assisting a shopper.

The woman was going to a Duck's game, and trying to figure out which PINK sweatshirt she wanted to get. She was extremely indecisive and so I told her which one I liked.

"I think the green one looks better," I said.

Still indecisive, so I said.

"You know what, let's see it on you."

I took it off the hanger, then put it over her head on top of what she was already wearing. She was giggling the entire time, as she tried to get her arms through the sleeves and from over her face.

I looked at her for a second, then confirmed what I had already thought.

"Well it definitely looks the best on you, and you said you like how this one feels. This is the one."

She thanked me, and after helping her I had something to do in the back. When I came out, she was in line at the register ready to check out.

I noticed her mainly because she was looking at me. I don't just mean in my direction, she was looking directly into my eyes and had this huge grin on her face.

That's how you look at the interviewer, give or take the massive grin. If she's reading this by the way, I want you to know you're one of my top 10 favorite customers. Come back anytime.

Besides eye contact, you should be relaxed and comfortable in your body language.

Don't Need It

Most people go and get a job out of need, but you don't want to act like you need it. The need for anything, gets in the way of everything.

Accept right now that if you don't end up getting this job, it's completely fine. When you don't need something, you can then relax and just enjoy yourself.

In my interview I enjoyed myself. I didn't need the job, so I brought that attitude in with me. I was having fun answering questions, while keeping everyone laughing with conversation, just having a grand old time.

Chapter 7

Post Interview

"Your success is your responsibility. Take the initiative, do the work, and persist to the end."

Though the interview is over with, we're still not done.

Persistence is key. Don't be annoying, but at the same time don't let them forget about you.

Also, you didn't read it in this book but....you can list friends as references. When I applied, my references were business owners and people high up who were a little hard to get a hold of. So, naturally they weren't able to speak with some of the people I listed.

And since in my case they called every reference, I had to go in and change them before they could hire me. Since I couldn't think of anyone else, I put down a relative, friend, and an acquaintance. They were able to successfully speak with each one of these new people, and apparently they liked what they had to say.

It's not like they call and ask

"You're not one of his family member's are you?"

Chapter 8

Conclusion

"There is no real ending. It's just the place where you stop the story."
-Frank Herbert

Using the ideas in this book, you should do fine come time for your next interview. And hopefully you've thoroughly enjoyed some of the stories I've shared of my experiences.

It's not over yet. Keep reading, I have thrown in some bonuses solely for your entertainment. Including an extremely interesting story about a trans-sexual. Also I've left the following pictures for your viewing pleasure.

Me trying on the wings

Some cake I had at 5 in the morning

Frequent Things I'm Told

If you ever get to meet me in person, feel free to ask me about anything not covered in this book, but here I am just going to answer the most common questions and comments I get repeatedly on a daily basis. I've added this section for your entertainment, besides the many stories I've shared throughout the rest of this book.

Questions and comments:

- **Dude, I know why you got this job!**

That's cool, but I can tell you're probably wrong.

- **You look like Pharrell, do you get that a lot?**

This is about the 18th time I've heard that today, yes.

- **Do you work here?**

No, I just love to come in and fold thongs everyday (sarcasm).

- **They hire guys here?**

Gotta love equal opportunity laws.

- **You look like that guy who sings the "happy" song, I can't think of his name....**

Say it....say it out loud (Twilight reference).

- **You must get all the phone numbers, huh?**

I literally have to ask for them.

- **Do you guys sell toe socks here?**

No.

- **I appreciate a guy working here.**

Why thank you, that one was nice.

- **Is this like, your dream job?**

It's retail.

- **Can you do fittings?**

No. The closest I've come to doing a fitting is when I was in the PINK room one day and this girl in her late teens came up and asked me to check what bra size she was.

Weird Things I've Heard:

Here are a few of the strangest things I've heard at random around the store:

-Context: Mother talking to daughter about Ultimate Yoga pants.
"They're reversible! You'll never have to do laundry again!"

-Context: Woman holding up a pair of panties
"I bet these will fit my ass"

-Context: Trans-sexual woman to me.
"I love you."

That last one is probably the most memorable to me.

An Additional Story

Here's a story I wanted to tell, but just didn't really know where I could put it:

This story is about my encounter with a trans-sexual. It all started as a normal day of fixing things, then she came in. Or at least I thought she.

Now before I found out that this woman was previously a man, she had asked about yoga pants. She was with her friend, who I am unsure was also trans-sexual or not. I'm not too good at telling.

Anyway, I was already in that area, so I showed her the yoga pants we had. She looked, then asked for a kind we don't have.

We started walking out of the room, when things got weird.

All of a sudden this woman just starts rapid fire asking me random questions one after the other.

"They let guys work here?"

"Are you tired?"

"Are you on drugs?"

She paused for a second, then she said it. She whispered, and I quote.

"I love you."

My eyes went big. I was in shock and didn't know what to do. How should you respond to something like that?

This time, however I was able to quickly recover from what I had just witnessed and excused myself. I brought over another co-worker and had her take her.

And here's the thing…..as soon as I handed her off to my co-worker, she started acting completely normal with her!

I quickly forgot about it, as I was just happy to be done with it and went back to what I was doing before. On her way out 10 minutes later, she looked over at me and yelled while grinning

"Bye friend."